BURN AFTER WRITING

A SIN JOURNAL

This journal belongs to:

BURN AFTER WRITING: A SIN JOURNAL

ISBN-13: 978-0692566398 (Scroll Media)
ISBN-10: 0692566392

Burn After Writing: A Sin Journal is produced by Scroll Media.
Visit Scroll Media for more custom journals.

Scroll Media Company
www.scrollmedia.com

Scroll Bookstore
www.scrollbookstore.com

Printed in the United States of America.

PURPOSE

Everyone has regrets. Not everyone faces them.

This tool is designed to help you organize your thoughts and tackle age-old sins that keep you awake at night. While your God (if you have one) may have his or her own way to help you deal with your past, it doesn't hurt to face it head on and tackle repentance and forgiveness.

This journal won't do it for you. This is not a tool to get out of having to say you're sorry, or to avoid making amends. This is to help you organize past mistakes to help you finally see a way to making corrections and finding peace.

This is not going to replace therapy, either, but even therapy often encourages people to be honest with themselves about their past and seek out those they have hurt in past situations, in order to create that bridge to forgiveness we all seek in our lives.

Nobody's perfect, but at least you can live cleanly by saying you did everything you could to make things right, as you're able to, and then forgive yourself in the long run.

How this Works

We make excuses for our mistakes, and unfortunately the very excuses we use to justify our behavior are often the very stumbling blocks that keep us from taking the steps to correct the situation and let it go.

This journal is only a tool. It can't bring you peace, but it might help you create a gameplan to make amends and let the past fade from your heart.

Use each entry to log something you reget, a past action that harmed someone else or even yourself, so be honest if you hold guilt for something you did, even to yourself -- anything that you can't let go.

DON'T write down all the excuses you've used.

DON'T fill up the page with how someone else hurt you. While other people might have abused you, that isn't what creates guilt in our hearts. Blaming yourself (for real or perceived faults) is what most often creates the pain that won't let us live in peace. This is about your behavior, not theirs.

So be honest, and keep to the real reason for each sin.

Believe it or not, peace isn't found when someone we hate asks our forgiveness, but when we learn to forgive them, and ourselves, for our past.

THE STEPS

STEP ONE - Read every question, put aside any emotions that suddenly well up within you, and really think as objectively as possible about the situation. Face each question humbly.

STEP TWO - Be honest about your missteps. This isn't about correcting others' misbchavior, but about finding atonement for your own, so in each situation, ask only what you did wrong.

STEP THREE - Avoid excuses. They're what keep us wrapped up in pain. "Well it's his fault." "*She* did it to me." "They should ask *me* for forgiveness!" These statements might be true, but you can't control others' behavior, only your own, so step up to the plate and clean up your own past. You might be surprised how freeing that can be.

STEP FOUR - Correct what you can, plot out steps to make amends and penance. If you honestly can't amend, (i.e. the person is dead, or attempting to make amends would make the situation worse), then say so. Then you have to CHOOSE to forgive yourself, with or without their forgiveness.

STEP FIVE - When you finish filling up this book, start a small fire, in your yard or a barbecue, or go camping to be alone. Create your own ceremony, read each sin, forgive yourself, and then burn it.

Commit

I am human like everyone else,
and my mistakes do not make me special.

I have sinned against others,
and it has brought me pain and regret.

I can't change the past,
but I can change my present and future.

I will do what I can today to make up
for yesterday's mistakes.

I will be humble, admit my wrongdoing
to those I hurt, and ask forgiveness.

For sins I cannot amend, I will release to the
changelessness of time, and let them go.

I refuse to cling any longer to a past
I cannot change, when I have done all I can
to correct what once I made wrong.

I embrace clean living today,
and I choose to embrace my own forgiveness.

I FORGIVE ME.

SIN 01

Q1

In one to two sentences, describe what happened, whom your hurt and how. Be brief, avoid details.

Q2

What was your reasoning for your behavior at the time?

Q3

When/how did you realize you were wrong?

Q4

Have you made penance?

Q5

If you made your penance, how did you do it? Was it enough? If you haven't, why haven't you?

Q6

If you haven't made penance, write out one way in which you can. If you have made penance, but don't feel it was enough, can you do more? Why or why not?

Q7

Write what it will take to do everything you possibly can to make penance. Outline your steps, then act. If you've done all you can, say so.

SIN 02

Q1

In one to two sentences, describe what happened, whom your hurt and how. Be brief, avoid details.

Q2

What was your reasoning for your behavior at the time?

Q3

When/how did you realize you were wrong?

Q4

Have you made penance?

Q5

If you made your penance, how did you do it? Was it enough? If you haven't, why haven't you?

Q6

If you haven't made penance, write out one way in which you can. If you have made penance, but don't feel it was enough, can you do more? Why or why not?

Q7

Write what it will take to do everything you possibly can to make penance. Outline your steps, then act. If you've done all you can, say so.

SIN 03

Q1

In one to two sentences, describe what happened, whom your hurt and how. Be brief, avoid details.

Q2

What was your reasoning for your behavior at the time?

Q3

When/how did you realize you were wrong?

Q4

Have you made penance?

Q5

If you made your penance, how did you do it? Was it enough? If you haven't, why haven't you?

Q6

If you haven't made penance, write out one way in which you can. If you have made penance, but don't feel it was enough, can you do more? Why or why not?

Q7

Write what it will take to do everything you possibly can to make penance. Outline your steps, then act. If you've done all you can, say so.

SIN 04

Q1

In one to two sentences, describe what happened, whom your hurt and how. Be brief, avoid details.

Q2

What was your reasoning for your behavior at the time?

Q3

When/how did you realize you were wrong?

Q4

Have you made penance?

Q5

If you made your penance, how did you do it? Was it enough? If you haven't, why haven't you?

Q6

If you haven't made penance, write out one way in which you can. If you have made penance, but don't feel it was enough, can you do more? Why or why not?

Q7

Write what it will take to do everything you possibly can to make penance. Outline your steps, then act. If you've done all you can, say so.

SIN 05

Q1

In one to two sentences, describe what happened, whom your hurt and how. Be brief, avoid details.

Q2

What was your reasoning for your behavior at the time?

Q3

When/how did you realize you were wrong?

Q4

Have you made penance?

Q5

If you made your penance, how did you do it? Was it enough? If you haven't, why haven't you?

Q6

If you haven't made penance, write out one way in which you can. If you have made penance, but don't feel it was enough, can you do more? Why or why not?

Q7

Write what it will take to do everything you possibly can to make penance. Outline your steps, then act. If you've done all you can, say so.

SIN 06

Q1

In one to two sentences, describe what happened, whom your hurt and how. Be brief, avoid details.

Q2

What was your reasoning for your behavior at the time?

Q3

When/how did you realize you were wrong?

Q4

Have you made penance?

Q5

If you made your penance, how did you do it? Was it enough? If you haven't, why haven't you?

Q6

If you haven't made penance, write out one way in which you can. If you have made penance, but don't feel it was enough, can you do more? Why or why not?

Q7

Write what it will take to do everything you possibly can to make penance. Outline your steps, then act. If you've done all you can, say so.

SIN 07

Q1

In one to two sentences, describe what happened, whom your hurt and how. Be brief, avoid details.

Q2

What was your reasoning for your behavior at the time?

Q3

When/how did you realize you were wrong?

Q4

Have you made penance?

Q5

If you made your penance, how did you do it? Was it enough? If you haven't, why haven't you?

Q6

If you haven't made penance, write out one way in which you can. If you have made penance, but don't feel it was enough, can you do more? Why or why not?

Q7

Write what it will take to do everything you possibly can to make penance. Outline your steps, then act. If you've done all you can, say so.

SIN 08

Q1

In one to two sentences, describe what happened, whom your hurt and how. Be brief, avoid details.

Q2

What was your reasoning for your behavior at the time?

Q3

When/how did you realize you were wrong?

Q4

Have you made penance?

Q5

If you made your penance, how did you do it? Was it enough? If you haven't, why haven't you?

Q6

If you haven't made penance, write out one way in which you can. If you have made penance, but don't feel it was enough, can you do more? Why or why not?

Q7

Write what it will take to do everything you possibly can to make penance. Outline your steps, then act. If you've done all you can, say so.

SIN 09

Q1

In one to two sentences, describe what happened, whom your hurt and how. Be brief, avoid details.

Q2

What was your reasoning for your behavior at the time?

Q3

When/how did you realize you were wrong?

Q4

Have you made penance?

Q5

If you made your penance, how did you do it? Was it enough? If you haven't, why haven't you?

Q6

If you haven't made penance, write out one way in which you can. If you have made penance, but don't feel it was enough, can you do more? Why or why not?

Q7

Write what it will take to do everything you possibly can to make penance. Outline your steps, then act. If you've done all you can, say so.

SIN 10

Q1

In one to two sentences, describe what happened, whom your hurt and how. Be brief, avoid details.

Q2

What was your reasoning for your behavior at the time?

Q3

When/how did you realize you were wrong?

Q4

Have you made penance?

Q5

If you made your penance, how did you do it? Was it enough? If you haven't, why haven't you?

Q6

If you haven't made penance, write out one way in which you can. If you have made penance, but don't feel it was enough, can you do more? Why or why not?

Q7

Write what it will take to do everything you possibly can to make penance. Outline your steps, then act. If you've done all you can, say so.

SIN 11

Q1

In one to two sentences, describe what happened, whom your hurt and how. Be brief, avoid details.

Q2

What was your reasoning for your behavior at the time?

Q3

When/how did you realize you were wrong?

Q4

Have you made penance?

Q5

If you made your penance, how did you do it? Was it enough? If you haven't, why haven't you?

Q6

If you haven't made penance, write out one way in which you can. If you have made penance, but don't feel it was enough, can you do more? Why or why not?

Q7

Write what it will take to do everything you possibly can to make penance. Outline your steps, then act. If you've done all you can, say so.

SIN 12

Q1

In one to two sentences, describe what happened, whom your hurt and how. Be brief, avoid details.

Q2

What was your reasoning for your behavior at the time?

Q3

When/how did you realize you were wrong?

Q4

Have you made penance?

Q5

If you made your penance, how did you do it? Was it enough? If you haven't, why haven't you?

Q6

If you haven't made penance, write out one way in which you can. If you have made penance, but don't feel it was enough, can you do more? Why or why not?

Q7

Write what it will take to do everything you possibly can to make penance. Outline your steps, then act. If you've done all you can, say so.

I will start a fire on this date:

____

I will read the commitment.

I will accept others' forgiveness,
and will not dismiss it when offered.

I will let go of those whom do not forgive me,
or with whom I cannot reasonably make amends.

I will forgive myself,
with or without their forgiveness.

I will commit to letting these sins pass from my
heart, learn from them, and allow peace to reign.

More from Scroll

www.scrollmedia.com - scrollbookstore.com

JOURNALS
Reflections: A Beginner's Journal
The NoteBible - www.notebible.com
Living&Moving - www.livingandmoving.net
Yankee Bugle - www.YankeeBugle.com

FICTION
Last Battle: Dusk of Xanthar
Stardusk

POETRY
Roses & Ravens: Search for Something

45281876R00020

Printed in Poland
by Amazon Fulfillment
Poland Sp. z o.o., Wrocław